WEEKLY **WR** READER®
EARLY LEARNING LIBRARY

Our Country's Holidays/
Las fiestas de nuestra nación

Martin Luther King Jr. Day/ Día de Martin Luther King Jr.

by/por Sheri Dean

author/l   opment

Please visit our web site at: www.earlyliteracy.cc
For a free color catalog describing Weekly Reader® Early Learning Library's list
of high-quality books, call 1-877-445-5824 (USA) or 1-800-387-3178 (Canada).
Weekly Reader® Early Learning Library's fax: (414) 336-0164.

Library of Congress Cataloging-in-Publication Data available upon request from publisher.
Fax (414) 336-0157 for the attention of the Publishing Records Department.

ISBN 0-8368-6520-0 (lib. bdg.)
ISBN 0-8368-6527-8 (softcover)

This edition first published in 2006 by
Weekly Reader® Early Learning Library
A Member of the WRC Media Family of Companies
330 West Olive Street, Suite 100
Milwaukee, WI 53212 USA

Copyright © 2006 by Weekly Reader® Early Learning Library

Managing editor: Valerie J. Weber
Art direction: Tammy West
Cover design and page layout: Kami Strunsee
Picture research: Cisley Celmer
Translators: Tatiana Acosta and Guillermo Gutiérrez

Picture credits: Cover, © Francis Miller/Time & Life Pictures/Getty Images; pp. 5, 9, 15, 17, 21
© AP/Wide World Photos; p. 7 © Diana Walker/Time & Life Pictures/Getty Images; p. 11 © Robert W.
Kelley/Time & Life Pictures/Getty Images; p. 13 © Delphine Fawundu/SuperStock; p. 19 © Vicky
Kasala/The Image Bank/Getty Images

Printed in the United States of America

1 2 3 4 5 6 7 8 9 10 09 08 07 06

Note to Educators and Parents

Reading is such an exciting adventure for young children! They are beginning to integrate their oral language skills with written language. To encourage children along the path to early literacy, books must be colorful, engaging, and interesting; they should invite the young reader to explore both the print and the pictures.

In *Our Country's Holidays*, children learn how the holidays they celebrate in their families and communities are observed across our nation. Using lively photographs and simple prose, each title explores a different national holiday and explains why it is significant.

Each book is specially designed to support the young reader in the reading process. The familiar topics are appealing to young children and invite them to read — and reread — again and again. The full-color photographs and enhanced text further support the student during the reading process.

In addition to serving as wonderful picture books in schools, libraries, homes, and other places where children learn to love reading, these books are specifically intended to be read within an instructional guided reading group. This small group setting allows beginning readers to work with a fluent adult model as they make meaning from the text. After children develop fluency with the text and content, the book can be read independently. Children and adults alike will find these books supportive, engaging, and fun!

— Susan Nations, M.Ed., author, literacy coach,
and consultant in literacy development

Nota para los maestros y los padres

¡Leer es una aventura tan emocionante para los niños pequeños! A esta edad están comenzando a integrar su manejo del lenguaje oral con el lenguaje escrito. Para animar a los niños en el camino de la lectura incipiente, los libros deben ser coloridos, estimulantes e interesantes; deben invitar a los jóvenes lectores a explorar la letra impresa y las ilustraciones.

Con la serie *Las fiestas de nuestra nación* los jóvenes lectores aprenderán que las fiestas que sus familias y sus comunidades celebran son días especiales en todo el país. Mediante vistosas fotografías y textos sencillos, cada libro explora una fiesta nacional diferente y explica por qué es importante.

Cada libro está especialmente diseñado para ayudar a los jóvenes lectores en el proceso de lectura. Los temas familiares llaman la atención de los niños y los invitan a leer — y releer — una y otra vez. Las fotografías a todo color y el tamaño de la letra ayudan aún más al estudiante en el proceso de lectura.

Además de servir como maravillosos libros ilustrados en escuelas, bibliotecas, hogares y otros lugares donde los niños aprenden a amar la lectura, estos libros han sido especialmente concebidos para ser leídos en un grupo de lectura guiada. Este contexto permite que los lectores incipientes trabajen con un adulto que domina la lectura mientras van determinando el significado del texto. Una vez que los niños dominan el texto y el contenido, el libro puede ser leído de manera independiente. ¡Estos libros les resultarán útiles, estimulantes y divertidos a niños y a adultos por igual!

— Susan Nations, M.Ed., autora/tutora de alfabetización/
consultora de desarrollo de la lectura

Martin Luther King Jr. Day celebrates the life of Martin Luther King Jr. He worked hard to make sure everyone was treated the same.

━ ━ ━ ━ ━ ━ ━ ━ ━ ━ ━ ━ ━ ━ ━ ━ ━

El Día de Martin Luther King Jr. se conmemora la vida de Martin Luther King Jr., que se esforzó para lograr que todas las personas fueran tratadas de la misma manera.

In 1986, Congress said we should all celebrate King and his work on the third Monday in January. President Ronald Reagan signed papers making that day a holiday across the country.

En 1986, el Congreso dijo que, el tercer lunes de enero, todos debemos honrar a King y a su obra. El presidente Ronald Reagan firmó los papeles que hicieron de esta fecha un día de fiesta nacional.

When King was a boy, many white people thought they were better than black people. Sometimes they treated these African Americans badly.

Cuando King era niño, muchas personas blancas se creían mejores que las personas negras. A veces, esas personas trataban mal a los afroamericanos.

African Americans had to live in certain parts of town. They had to go to black schools.   Some African Americans could not vote.

━ ━ ━ ━ ━ ━ ━ ━ ━ ━ ━ ━ ━ ━ ━ ━

Los afroamericanos tenían que vivir en ciertas zonas de la ciudad. Tenían que ir a escuelas para personas negras. Algunos no podían votar.

King had a dream. He wanted to change this. He wanted everyone to live, learn, and play together.

King tenía un sueño. Quería que las cosas cambiaran. Deseaba que todos vivieran, estudiaran y jugaran juntos.

King spoke to many people about his dream. He led marches to show that people wanted to change.

King le habló de su sueño a muchas personas. Realizó marchas para demostrar que la gente deseaba cambiar.

14

King did not believe in fighting. He did not believe hurting people would help his dream.

- - - - - - - - - - - - - - -

King no creía en las peleas. Pensaba que hacer daño a los demás no ayudaría a que su sueño se hiciera realidad.

16

KEEP
THE
DREAM
ALIVE

King did change how people thought. He helped people to be treated the same.

King cambió la manera de pensar de las personas. Ayudó a que todos fueran tratados de la misma manera.

On Martin Luther King Jr. Day , we learn about his life. We write about King and draw pictures. We give speeches about him. We think about how we can help people too.

El Día de Martin Luther King Jr. estudiamos su vida. Escribimos cosas sobre él y hacemos dibujos. Damos charlas sobre este hombre. También pensamos en lo que podemos hacer para ayudar a los demás.

21

Glossary

African American — a person of African background who lives in the United States

Congress — the part of the government that makes laws

march — an event when people walk together to show their support for a goal

Glosario

afroamericano — persona de origen africano que vive en Estados Unidos

Congreso — parte del gobierno que hace las leyes

marcha — ocasión en la que muchas personas caminan juntas para demostrar su apoyo a una meta común

For More Information/
Más información

Books

A Picture Book of Martin Luther King. David Adler
(Live Oak Media)
Martin's Big Words: The Life of Dr. Martin Luther King, Jr.
Doreen Rappaport (Jump At the Sun)

Libros

El día de Martin Luther King, Jr/Martin Luther King Day.
Historias de Fiestas/Holiday Histories (series). Mir Tamim
Ansary (Heinemann)

Web Sites/Páginas web

Martin Luther King, Jr. Day
Día de Martin Luther King, Jr.
www.holidays.net/mlk
Hear King's most famous speech and learn about his life and the
way we celebrate his work.
Escucha el discurso más famoso de King y conoce su vida y cómo
honramos su obra.

Index

African
  Americans 8
blacks 8
change 12,
  14, 18
Congress 6
dream 12,
  14, 16
fighting 16
helping 20
marches 14

Reagan, Ronald
  6
schools 10
voting 10
whites 8

Índice

afroamericanos 8
ayudar 20
blancos 8
cambio 12,
  14, 18
Congreso 6
escuelas 10
marchas 14
negros 8
pelear 16

Reagan,
  Ronald 6
sueño 12, 14,
  16
votar 10

About the Author

Sheri Dean is a school librarian in Milwaukee, Wisconsin. She was an elementary school teacher for fourteen years. She enjoys introducing books and information to curious children and adults.

Información sobre la autora

Sheri Dean trabaja como bibliotecaria en Milwaukee, Wisconsin. Durante catorce años, fue maestra de primaria. A Sheri le gusta proporcionar información y libros novedosos a niños y adultos con ganas de aprender.